# PREPARING FOR PROMOTION, TENURE, AND ANNUAL REVIEW

# PREPARING FOR PROMOTION, TENURE, AND ANNUAL REVIEW

## A Faculty Guide

### SECOND EDITION

### Robert M. Diamond
The National Academy for Academic Leadership

ANKER PUBLISHING COMPANY, INC.

Published by Jossey-Bass
A Wiley Imprint
989 Market Street, San Francisco, CA 94103-1741   www.josseybass.com

Jossey-Bass books and products are available through most bookstores. To contact Jossey-Bass directly call our Customer Care Department within the U.S. at 800-956-7739, outside the U.S. at 317-572-3986, or fax 317-572-4002.

Jossey-Bass also publishes its books in a variety of electronic formats. Some content that appears in print may not be available in electronic books.

ISBN-13 978-1-882982-72-1
ISBN-10 1-882982-72-X

Printed in the United States of America
FIRST EDITION
PB Printing          10 9 8 7 6 5 4 3 2 1

## ABOUT THE AUTHOR

ROBERT M. DIAMOND is research professor of education at Syracuse University and president of the National Academy for Academic Leadership. He was formerly assistant vice chancellor, director of the Center for Instructional Development, and professor of instructional design, development and evaluation, and higher education at Syracuse University, where he directed the National Project on Institutional Priorities and Faculty Rewards funded by the Carnegie Foundation for the Advancement of Teaching, the Fund for the Improvement of Postsecondary Education, the Lilly Endowment, and the Pew Charitable Trusts. He coauthored the 1987 National Study of Teaching Assistants, the 1992, 1994, and 1996 National Studies on the Perceived Balance Between Research and Undergraduate Teaching, and was responsible for the design and implementation of Syracuse University's award-winning high school/college transition program, Project Advance. He also co-directed the Syracuse University Focus on Teaching Project. Dr. Diamond has published extensively and is a consultant to colleges and universities throughout the world. His publications include *Aligning Faculty Rewards with Institutional Mission: Statements, Policies, and Guidelines* (1999), *Serving on Promotion, Tenure, and Faculty Review Committees: A Faculty Guide* (2002), and *Designing & Assessing Courses & Curricula: A Practical Guide* (1997). He is editor of *Field Guide to Academic Leadership* (2002) and co-editor of the two-volume series *The Disciplines Speak* (1995 & 2000).

# TABLE OF CONTENTS

## Part II
## Resources

# PREFACE

This new edition of *Preparing for Promotion, Tenure, and Annual Review* contains a number of additional resources not included in the previous version, materials that are designed to assist you as you prepare for a major professional review. If you are using technology in your teaching, you will find suggestions on how you might best document these activities. There are also expanded sections and resources on teaching and on advising, on how to best document your role and impact when you are part of a team, and a discussion on how the issue of collegiality might be addressed. In addition, the section on scholarship has been greatly expanded to provide you with a rationale and guidelines for describing scholarly, professional, and creative work that is traditional, nontraditional, or applied. The approach that is suggested also has the advantage of working across all disciplines and at all institutions.

To assist you further, references have been updated and new resources identified. As with the earlier edition, this book has been developed on the basic premise that, as the candidate, you can play a major role in ensuring that the review process will be fair and that you will provide your review committee with the best documentation possible.

While the focus of this book is on promotion, tenure, and annual review, it should be noted that a growing number of faculty are on multiyear, nontenure-track appointments. If you are in one of these positions you can expect to be evaluated using many of the same criteria for teaching and service as discussed in this guide.

*Robert M. Diamond*
*December 2003*

# Acknowledgments

I would like to thank the following colleagues for their excellent feedback and suggestions on this guide and its previous edition: Bronwyn Adam, Lou Albert, Bill Bayliss, Paula Brownlee, Ron Cavanagh, Kim Dittus, Sandra Elman, Don Ely, Jim Gardner, Rachael Hendrickson, Sam Hope, Bob Jensen, Bill Laidlaw, Gene Rice, Robert Rubinstein, Rich Sours, Toni Toland, Dan Wheeler, Mark Whitney, and Assate Zerai. I would also like to thank Susan Anker and Ron Pynn for their support and outstanding suggestions as this revised edition was being developed.

This guide was initially developed as part of the Syracuse University National Project on Institutional Priorities and Faculty Rewards funded by the Carnegie Foundation for the Advancement of Teaching, the Lilly Endowment, the Pew Charitable Trusts, and the Fund for the Improvement of Postsecondary Education.

# Introduction

Evaluation of faculty occurs on every college campus throughout the country. Every faculty member can expect to be evaluated on an ongoing basis throughout his or her career. For many, faculty evaluation will be an annual event; for others, assessment occurs at key times in their careers. While this is a challenging and anxious experience, faculty evaluation need not be unfair or inappropriate. The purpose of this book is to make the evaluation process fairer and somewhat less challenging, and certainly more survivable.

As a faculty member, you can anticipate annual reviews, reviews for promotion and tenure, and, on a growing number of campuses, post-tenure reviews. This process can, at times, be difficult, often confusing, and stressful. However, with an average faculty member requiring a total investment of over $2,000,000 during his or her career, it is no wonder that trustees, political leaders, and the general public are calling for more accountability and major improvements with the faculty review and assessment process.

While typically your first formal review by a full faculty committee will be for promotion, there are instances where this review can be for both promotion and tenure. As important as these reviews are, you may find the process on your campus to be unclear and confusing, with different, well-meaning individuals giving you differing and often conflicting advice. Fortunately, the process at many institutions is improving. In addition, by being proactive, by asking the right questions, by reading the right materials, and by seeking the advice of those who have been through the process or who are serving on your review committee, you can help ensure that your evaluation will be both fair and appropriate.

This guide is intended to assist you in preparing for these reviews. Also keep in mind that the materials you collect for your annual review can provide a solid base for the more detailed documents you will be producing for your tenure and promotion committee.

Included here are materials appropriate for faculty at large universities and small colleges, public and private institutions, and unionized campuses. Settings do indeed vary; however, the questions that need to be considered and the materials you will need to collect are basically the same across all contexts. What will vary considerably are the policies and procedures followed, the criteria applied to evaluate your work, the weight given to specific activities, and the extent to which assistance is provided along the way through formal and informal institutional channels or networks.

A number of initiatives are underway on campuses and in national associations to make the promotion and tenure process fairer to candidates and more closely aligned with the priorities of departments and institutions. Guidelines are being clarified, techniques for documenting faculty work are being developed, and, in a number of departments, experienced and respected faculty members are being asked to work with new faculty members as mentors. In addition, there is a growing body of literature on the subject of faculty evaluation and assessment.

As a candidate for promotion or tenure, perhaps the most important thing for you to realize is that there are a number of things you can do, almost from the first day of your appointment, to improve your chances of a positive review. The more you know about the process and timeline that will be followed on your campus and in your department, the criteria that will be used, and the ways in which you can document your accomplishments, the greater your chances for success. You have an important role to play in determining the focus of your review and in selecting those materials that will be reviewed by the promotion and/or tenure committee.

In addition, as part of the review process, you have the opportunity of educating your committee about new developments in your discipline, new approaches to teaching, and other topics that can improve the fairness of the review process.

This guide has been developed to assist you by enumerating important questions you should ask and the issues you should consider as you approach your review. Included are some suggestions concerning the materials that you will submit for review. You will also find specific examples illustrating how you might document the impact of your professional work as well as a review of the data and support materials you could provide. Keep in mind that there is no single format or best approach. Every promotion and tenure review is bound by its context. Yours will be determined by the guidelines and procedures of your department, school/college, or institution; by the campus culture; by the specific assignments you have undertaken; and by your own set of interests and priorities. In this book the focus is on process—what you can do to make a better case for why you should be promoted or tenured.

# PART I
## PROCESS

# 1

## PLANNING AHEAD

The more complete the information you have about the promotion, tenure, and annual review process at your institution, the better. As you read this book, it is important to keep in mind that criteria and procedures vary from institution to institution, from discipline to discipline, and from department to department. While in a larger institution there may be several committees involved (often at the department, school/college, and institution level), in a smaller institution there is apt to be a single promotion and tenure committee reporting directly to the provost, campus dean, or academic vice president.

The materials you need to collect for your annual review can be a part of the documents you provide for promotion and tenure. Keep in mind throughout the process of preparing your portfolio—and this is most important—that at some point in the process those reviewing your materials will be from other academic disciplines. Don't assume that the reader knows your field or is familiar with the research you're discussing or building on. You will also find a difference in focus between promotion and tenure committees. While promotion committees tend to base their decision on past accomplishments, tenure committees will consider both past performance and your long-term potential at your institution, that is, what you can contribute to the unit and to the institution in the years ahead. Start early to prepare for your review. Long before the actual date of your final review, there are a number of steps you can take. Begin by collecting key information.

## KNOW THE RULES: PROCEDURES AND CRITERIA

### What You Should Know

Shortly after your faculty appointment, you should begin to gather information in five general areas.

1) *The review process in your unit*

   - Is there an annual review procedure? Is this a formal or informal review process? What are you expected to provide? What factors are being considered?

   - Is there a more comprehensive three-year review? How is it similar or different in process and practice from the tenure review?

2) *The type of documentation the committee will expect*

   - What materials will the committee expect you to provide to document your teaching, research on scholarship, and service activities?

   - If a professional or teaching portfolio is expected or encouraged, what should be included, and how should it be organized and presented?

   - Will you be asked to provide copies of publications? Will you be asked to provide published reviews of these publications? Will you be asked to solicit other reviews?

   - Should you provide letters of support, and, if so, from whom and how many?

   - Should you provide a list of references, and, if so, when?

   - How much material should be presented and on what timeline?

   - Find out if important new materials can still be provided after the review process has begun. If this option is available it can be very important if you have works in progress or about to be published.

3) *The specific steps that will be followed by the committee(s)*

   - What steps will the committee follow, and what is the anticipated timeline? When will decisions be made?

- Will the committee interview other colleagues?

- Will documentation or assessment be requested from individuals outside the institution?

- How will these external reviewers be selected, and what will they be asked to do?

- Are you expected to provide nominations for outside reviewers? If so, select these individuals with great care, making sure that they hold positions that indicate recognition in their field in addition to disciplinary expertise.

4) *The criteria that will be used to assess the quality of the materials that are provided*

- Publications, for example, can be reviewed in many ways. Will the materials simply be counted using some formula for weighting, or will a sample be reviewed against a specific set of standards? How are different publications weighted? Which are the "valued" publications in your discipline and in your department?

- How will the quality of teaching or advising be determined, and how will the quality and significance of other professional activities be measured?

5) *The relative weighting of various activities*

- Is there a set formula for determining the importance of specific functions, or will these be considered on an individual basis according to assignment?

- Is there a standard approach for determining the relative weight of activities (for example, 40% on the quality of teaching, 40% research, and 20% service)?

Information of this nature may be provided to you by your department or program chair or by another designated mentor. At many institutions, the communication of most of this information is part of a formal three-year review process. If preparatory information is not provided to you, ask for it. Your institution or department may not have addressed some of these questions or issues. If that is the case, it will be up to you to prepare for the committee a file of materials that makes the best case for the quality of your work.

## DEALING WITH CHANGING GUIDELINES AND POLICIES

Keep in mind that policies or practices at your institution may change after your initial appointment. Be sure that you are informed of any modifications of criteria and procedures that apply to you. In some instances you may have the option of selecting either the criteria that were in place when you were appointed or the revised version. Make sure to pick the option that is best for you.

## KNOW THE PEOPLE AND THEIR ROLES

It is important to be aware of who will be on your various committees (usually determined months ahead), what academic units will be represented (very important if you are on a joint appointment), who the chair will be, and what role your department chair or dean will play. If you find a key gap in content expertise on your committee, don't be afraid to advocate for additional membership. It never hurts to ask the committee chair or its members for advice well in advance of submitting your materials.

## COLLECT OTHER USEFUL INFORMATION

There are several formal documents that will prove helpful to you as you begin to describe, define, and document the quality and significance of your work:

- Your institutional mission and vision statements
- Your school/college or departmental mission or priority statements
- A statement from your discipline describing the work of faculty in your field
- On unionized campuses, the sections of the collective bargaining agreement related to promotion and tenure procedures and criteria
- Regional accreditation standards (these associations and agencies are increasingly including promotion and tenure guidelines in their criteria)

## Mission and Vision Statements

The more closely your work relates to the stated mission and vision of your institution, school/college, or department, the more likely it is that greater weight will be applied to that work in your review. In recent years a growing number of institutions have clarified their mission statements with schools/colleges and departments describing their priorities in detail and relating their promotion, tenure, and merit guidelines to these priorities. It will be up to you to relate the materials you present to what the institution says it values, making the case for your work as a manifestation of institutional goals. Since department missions can vary significantly, explication of your practice as it relates to the priorities of your academic unit is important information for the committee to have.

## A Statement From Your Discipline

As you prepare your materials, remember that there are major differences among the disciplines, both in terms of faculty practice and methodology and in the language used to describe faculty work. These differences can be problematic when a faculty member comes up for review by colleagues from other disciplines, particularly if the work presented does not take the form of traditional research and publication. This problem was addressed in a document prepared for the American Historical Association by a committee established to address definitions of scholarship in history.

> This debate over priorities is not discipline-specific but extends across the higher education community. Nevertheless, each discipline has specific concerns and problems. For history, the privilege given to the monograph in promotion and tenure has led to the undervaluing of other activities central to the life of the discipline—writing textbooks, developing courses and curricula, documentary editing, museum exhibitions, and film projects to name but a few. (American Historical Association, 1993, ¶ 2)

To provide assistance in the assessment of faculty work, a number of discipline associations have participated in a project centered at Syracuse University (sponsored by the Carnegie Foundation for the Advancement of Teaching, the Fund for the Improvement of

Postsecondary Education, the Lilly Endowment, and the Pew Charitable Trusts) to develop comprehensive statements describing the scholarly and professional work in their respective fields. These statements provide valuable guidelines to faculty who must document for those outside of their fields the discipline-specific nature of scholarship. The completed statements from more than 25 disciplines can be found in a two-volume set, *The Disciplines Speak* (Diamond & Adam, 1995, 2000), published by the American Association for Higher Education. Included are statements from the following:

### Volume I

American Academy of Religion
American Chemical Society
American Historical Association
Association for Education in Journalism and
    Mass Communications
Association of American Geographers
Association to Advance Collegiate Schools of Business
Council of Administrators of Family and Consumer Sciences
Joint Policy Board for Mathematics
Landscape Architectural Accreditation Board
National Architectural Accrediting Board
National Association of Schools of Art and Design
National Association of Schools of Dance
National Association of Schools of Music
National Association of Schools of Theatre
National Office for Arts Accreditation in Higher Education

### Volume II

American Association of Colleges for Teacher Education
American Association of Colleges of Nursing
American Association of Medical Colleges (Status Report)
American Physical Society
American Psychological Association
American Society of Civil Engineers
Association of College and Research Libraries
Council on Social Work Education
Modern Language Association
National Council for Black Studies
National Women's Studies Association
Society for College Science Teachers

An excellent resource for candidates in the medical field is *Redefining Scholarship in Contemporary Academic Medicine* (Association of American Medical Colleges, 2000).

## Know Your Options

As a faculty member approaching promotion and tenure, there may be several options available to you. In an increasing number of institutions, faculty are being given the opportunity to negotiate the weighting that will be applied to their various activities (teaching, research, service, citizenship, outreach, etc.) prior to review. This practice acknowledges the individual differences of faculty assignments and the need to consider reviews on a case-by-case basis.

You may also have the option of taking a leave of absence or reduced teaching load in order to prepare for your review. In some situations there may be an option of stopping the tenure clock to provide you with adequate time to prepare your case. Investigate all of these options with your department chair or dean. Taking advantage of additional time to carefully prepare your case can make a significant difference in the outcome.

## The Collective Bargaining Agreement

If you work on a unionized campus, a review of the collective bargaining agreement can be helpful. Such contracts typically address evaluation procedures, specific timelines, and the composition of review committees, among other particulars. For a discussion of tenure prepared from the union perspective, see Chapter 6 in *Aligning Faculty Rewards with Institutional Mission* (Diamond, 1999).

## The Formal Appeal Process

Every institution has a formal appeal process to which faculty can turn for review of a negative decision. This process will usually be described in your faculty handbook or collective bargaining agreement. Even if you don't need it, you should know the process.

## DEVELOP A FOCUSED INTEREST IN A SPECIFIC LINE OF RESEARCH

Promotion and tenure committees look for evidence of sustained inquiry—of depth and long-term disciplinary commitment that centers and integrates one's professional work. It is important that you develop a specialty or area of expertise that is appropriate for your field and your long-term goals and that you can articulate clearly. As you move ahead, you will need to document the full scope of your activity and the significance of it. Focus on how your work is making a contribution to your field. If articles or research reports are appropriate, aim at having them published in refereed journals. If you are in the creative arts, have your work peer reviewed in exhibitions or by experts in the field. Consider developing presentations in your area of specialization for regional and national meetings. Conference papers are a good first step toward publication, often providing critical feedback that can lead to revision and successful journal submission. Also find ways of relating your work to your teaching, and, if possible, have students join you as you pursue your line of inquiry. Your documentation in this area will provide the basis for the committee's review of the scholarly/professional/creative dimension of your work.

## DOCUMENT SPECIAL ASSIGNMENTS

While most institutions try to avoid giving new faculty members assignments that constrain their ability to devote time to the more traditional activities of teaching, research, and publication, there are exceptions. You may be asked or even required to participate in specific projects, be involved in major course or curriculum design activities, or assume a number of administrative responsibilities. These can affect your promotion and tenure in three ways. First, such responsibilities can impinge on the range of activities that you can realistically perform. Second, such work can have an impact on the time you have available to conduct research, prepare publications, attempt innovations in your teaching, or perform service in your institution or community. Third, these activities can, under certain circumstances, be recognized as scholarly and professional work by your department. If a special assignment will not be recognized in your review and will impinge on your time to a significant degree, you should discuss with your department chair possibilities for adjusting your tenure clock (i.e., how many years you have before a formal review is required).

Request that the assignment and related expectations and activities be put in writing and filed in your personnel folder. Also, keep a copy in your own files. If there is agreement that this activity will be considered as your scholarship, make sure to get this statement in writing. If such assignments and conditions are included in your appointment letter, make sure that this document is also in your file. You may want to refer to them later and include them in your portfolio as you describe the focus of your work and the constraints under which you were working.

## COLLECT BASELINE DATA

In the years prior to your formal review for promotion or tenure, many events and experiences will provide opportunities for personal growth and professional development. Documenting those activities may prove to be invaluable as you approach tenure or promotion review. You may be asked to address a problem identified in your work, perhaps at the time of an earlier review. (Many institutions are now implementing a required, in-depth review of all faculty during their third year of appointment for the specific reason of helping them prepare for their tenure review.) You may want to experiment with some innovative instructional strategy in a class to address concerns you have, or you may make major changes in the content of a course for instructional improvement. In such instances, you will want to collect data on the problem before you do anything. Such baseline data might consist of student responses to the current curriculum, data from a student survey on your teaching, comments from alumni or employers, student grades and test results, attrition data, or any information that helps identify the problem you perceive.

If you are active in community-related projects, look for reports or surveys that articulate the problem you plan to address. There may also be articles in professional journals that provide a strong rationale for the work you want to pursue. All of these sources can be incorporated as documentation when you present your case. Look for data that can be useful as you attempt to show the positive impact your work has had. As you plan changes in your work with students or in your scholarship, you need to consider potential outcomes. You may want to ask yourself the questions, "If I am successful, what will change, how will it change, and how can I document this change?"

## RECOGNIZE THE UNIQUE CHALLENGES YOU MUST FACE

Most faculty serving on promotion and tenure committees will be comfortable with the documentation associated with research and scholarly publication. A growing number will also be familiar with the various means of assessing and documenting good teaching. There are, however, several areas where problems of multiple interpretations and values typically arise.

### Defining Scholarly and Professional Work

There is no single, agreed-upon definition of what is meant by the term "scholarship." Some disciplines avoid the word altogether, preferring instead "professional or creative work" or "intellectual contribution." Each discipline has its own definition, and it may not be articulated in a formal document. In order to help your reviewers understand the quality of your work, you may need to provide the committee with the definition of scholarship or professional work from your field. Disciplinary statements can support your rationale for the scholarly and professional nature of your work.

### New and Developing Disciplines

If you are in one of the newer academic areas such as women's studies or African-American studies, you face a unique challenge. In new disciplines, a research history or tradition may not exist, and publication outlets may be limited. In addition, much of the documentation that does exist may appear in nontraditional forms such as video, audio histories, or in publications that do not have clearly established traditions. Some committee members may be unfamiliar with your field. It will be up to you to provide them with a rationale and documentation that they can understand, appreciate, and assess. Find out how leading educators in your field on other campuses have addressed these issues and learn from them. Useful statements for both women's studies and African-American studies can be found in Volume II of *The Disciplines Speak* (Diamond & Adam, 2000).

### Interdisciplinary or Collaborative Work

Just as faculty in newer disciplines face challenges, so do the growing number of faculty involved in interdisciplinary or collaborative work. Increasing thought is being given to the assessment of work produced by coauthors, co-investigators, or teams that may consist of faculty from more than one discipline or experts from the community. While the overall success of your work will have to be documented, it will be your responsibility to describe and assess your role within the group and the impact that you had on the outcome of the collaboration. If you are working in an interdisciplinary context, take particular care to relate your work to your own discipline and to the priorities of your department and institution. See Resource 1 in Part II for a list of key questions you should address in your portfolio.

## Changes in Leadership

Appointment of a new department chair, dean, or administrator can precipitate a radical change in promotion and tenure policies or practices. Such changes can evolve over time or be quite sudden. Whenever significant change does occur, you need to pay particular attention to any new statements regarding promotion and tenure review. If new policies seem quite different from written statements in effect previously or from particular agreements you negotiated, address this difference with your department chair or unit head immediately. If a new policy is put in place, find out if you have the option to select the old or the new policy.

### RECOGNIZE THE IMPORTANCE OF INTERPERSONAL RELATIONSHIPS

Remember that promotion and tenure is a political process involving the attitudes and perceptions of committee members, argument and deliberation components, and formal and informal voting. Citizenship is becoming increasingly important as a criterion for tenure. Even with strong credentials, you may be refused tenure if you are perceived as being uncooperative or uninterested in working with colleagues in your department. This is not a time to champion unpopular causes or to appear unwilling to compromise. Resource 2 in Part II describes the characteristics a committee might look for when determining collegiality. For an in-depth discussion of the political nature of the faculty review process, see *Getting Tenure* by Whicker, Kronenfeld, and Strickland (1993).

## KEEP YOUR RÉSUMÉ UP-TO-DATE

Begin collecting materials for your dossier early, and update your résumé on a regular basis. From the day of your appointment, begin filing important documents that could prove useful later. As your file expands, you can begin organizing your materials in a number of ways. The materials you submit to the review committee will not include all of the documents and materials you collect. However, keep everything, including your annual review materials, until you need to decide what you will include. This strategy will provide you with a wide array of materials to select from later. Noting on an annual or semi-annual basis the titles and dates for courses taught, special assignments, papers, presentations, publications, and awards will keep your records complete and current. Deleting items later is much easier than trying to recall particulars four years down the road.

## GET HELP

As you start preparing your materials, ask a colleague to review for you the first complete draft, attending to both clarity and completeness. This person may be your mentor or another faculty member whose judgment you trust. It is particularly helpful to find a person who has served on a promotion and tenure committee at your institution. If you are on a campus where the initial committee is cross disciplinary, having someone from another department who is not familiar with your field look over your materials can be useful. These individuals can also help by identifying areas in which official policy and actual practice have diverged in recent history. Does institutional rhetoric reflect reality? Getting this anecdotal information is crucial to understanding the culture of your institution and how it affects promotion and tenure review.

## GETTING STARTED

The promotion and tenure review has three components: the documentation that the candidate provides, the material that the committee collects, and the process by which the committee reviews these materials and conducts its deliberations. A well-prepared faculty member can go a long way in making his or her case by providing a strong context and solid documentation for the committee to consider.

In the previous pages we noted the importance of knowing the rules and procedures that will be followed, the criteria that will be used, and the information you should collect. Almost immediately after being appointed you should begin the process of getting to know the people and procedures. Don't expect to be prodded by your chair or other faculty; it is up to you to take the initiative. You may be fortunate to be on a campus where a formal mentoring program is in place or where a faculty support (development) agency is available to provide you with guidelines and resources. If such a unit does exist, explore it (and its library), and find out how they may help. If ever there is a time to be proactive, this is it.

In the past, collecting and presenting your documentation, while not easy, was straightforward: teaching, research, and service. This is no longer the case. As a faculty member there is a good chance that you will be involved in a wide range of important activities, each of which should be included in your portfolio. You may find yourself involved in recruiting, representing your institution in the community, serving as a member of a team working on a course or curriculum design, or actively investigating new applications of technology in your field of study or in your teaching. While it will be up to you to select the specific focus of your scholarly, creative, or professional work that you wish to highlight, it is important that the portfolio you present includes quality documentation for each area in which you work. *Do not overlook anything.*

Begin by making a list of the various areas in which you are assigned or will be working. Review this outline on a regular basis and add to it as new activities arise. This list can provide you with the structure of the materials you provide the committee.

## Your Portfolio Is an Educational Tool

Keep in mind that your portfolio will have an educational role. You will use it to educate members of your committee (particularly if they are from other disciplines) on the importance and quality of your work and how your activities support the mission and vision of your institution. Committee members may not be as informed about the research on teaching and learning as you would hope. Don't assume anything.

## Know the Literature

While you will be up-to-date on the research in your field, you and members of your committee will most likely not be well versed in the research on teaching, learning, assessment, student development, advising, and so on. There are several resources that can quickly provide you with a solid foundation in each of these areas. Showing that what you are doing in your teaching, advising, and professional work is based on the literature will improve your portfolio as well as your standing with the evaluation committee. This recent research can only strengthen your presentation. Start with Gardiner (1994), *Redesigning Higher Education,* or Diamond (2002), *Field Guide to Academic Leadership* (especially Chapters 7, 8, 10, 11, 12, and 14). Both of these volumes are well written and to the point. They will provide you with reviews of the latest research in key areas and include excellent bibliographies and references.

## Stopping or Slowing Down the Tenure Clock

Most institutions with tenure try to avoid giving new faculty special assignments that may constrain their ability to devote time to the more traditional activities of research and publication. They are not always successful. Before committing to an assignment that may take you away from your major field of study (department chair, serving on a special task force or committee, etc.), explore the possibility of slowing down or stopping the tenure clock. Far too often, nontenured faculty accept the position of department chair only to find that it is impossible for them to meet the expectations of the position and their need to fulfill the scholarly requirements for tenure.

Your institution may provide the option of slowing down the tenure clock for personal or other professional reasons. Some campuses even offer the opportunity to move into a part-time tenure line for several years. Check what options exist on your campus. If you get an agreement to modify your timeline or to focus on a nontraditional area of research, get it in writing and provide it to your committee early in the review process.

# 2

# DOCUMENTING YOUR WORK

## THE SCOPE OF DOCUMENTATION

As noted in Chapter 1, the promotion and tenure review has three basic parts: the documentation the candidate provides, the materials the committee collects, and the review of this material by the committee. By structuring your materials carefully you make the work of the committee easier and you make your case by providing a strong context and solid documentary materials for the committee to consider.

Many descriptions of the work of faculty have been suggested as alternatives to the traditional three-part model of teaching, research, and service. One expanded taxonomy identifies the following as common discipline-based faculty activities (Gray, Adam, Diamond, Froh, & Yonai, 1994).

*Working with students in many different settings and using many different methods for:*

- Teaching undergraduates and graduates

- Advising pre-freshmen to postdoctoral fellows

*Citizenship (nondisciplinary):*

- Serving on departmental, school, or institutional committees

- Assuming leadership roles within the institution and in professional organizations

- Representing the institution on external committees, task forces, commissions, etc.

*Scholarly activity involving:*

- Research that leads to the production of intellectual and/or creative works

- Writing for publication, presentation, or performance

*Professional service through the application of:*

- Disciplinary expertise to assist the institution, citizen groups, government agencies, businesses, industry

Depending on the particular activities you present for review, it will be your committee's responsibility to determine if all the required elements are included and if the significance and quality of your work is documented. While the documentation of basic research and publication has become fairly standardized since the 1980s, demonstration of quality work in other domains has only recently received attention.

## DOCUMENTING SCHOLARSHIP

### What Scholarship Is

Ernest Boyer (1990), building on the work of Eugene Rice, proposed that colleges and universities move beyond the debate of teaching versus research and that the definition of scholarship be expanded to include:

- The scholarship of discovery: original research

- The scholarship of integration: the synthesizing and reintegration of knowledge

- The scholarship of application: professional practice

- The scholarship of teaching: the transformation of knowledge through teaching

While many institutions and disciplinary associations have used this model as the basis for their expanded approach to describing scholarship, others have modified the four classifications or included them within their own, often traditional, framework. If you are finding these terms in use at your institution and in the policies you are working with, a brief review of Boyer's work might prove most helpful.

Some disciplines, to reduce communication problems with those outside their field, have moved away from using the term "scholarship" and have replaced it with "creative or professional work" of faculty.

## WHAT MAKES IT SCHOLARSHIP?

Recognizing that the academy needs a way of describing the scholarly aspects of faculty work that communicates across disciplines, between programs and departments, and among institutions, it is helpful to focus on the common characteristics of scholarly processes and their outcomes.

To do this we build on two earlier publications. The first, *Recognizing Faculty Work* (Diamond & Adam, 1993), identifies six characteristics that typify scholarly processes and production:

- The activity requires a high level of discipline expertise.

- The activity breaks new ground or is innovative.

- The activity can be replicated or elaborated.

- The work and its results can be documented.

- The work and its results can be peer reviewed.

- The activity has significance or impact.

In the second, Charles E. Glassick, Mary Taylor Huber, and Gene I. Maeroff (1997), building on the earlier work of Ernest Boyer and Eugene Rice, suggest in *Scholarship Assessed* that six qualitative standards can be applied to scholarly work:

- Clear goals

- Adequate preparation

- Appropriate methods

- Significant results

- Effective presentation

- Reflective critique

*Recognizing Faculty Work* describes the *products* of scholarly, professional, or creative work, while Glassick, Huber, and Maeroff's approach focuses more on the *process* of scholarship. It is a combination of these two aspects—product and process—that provide a practical and functional way of describing and evaluating the scholarly work of faculty (see Table 2.1).

TABLE 2.1

## What Makes It Scholarship

An activity will be considered scholarly if it meets the following criteria:

1) The activity or work requires a high level of discipline-related expertise.

2) The activity or work is conducted in a scholarly manner with:
   - Clear goals
   - Adequate preparation
   - Appropriate methodology

3) The activity or work and its results are appropriately documented and disseminated. This reporting should include a reflective component that addresses the significance of the work, the process that was followed, and the outcomes of the research, inquiry, or activity.

4) The activity or work has significance beyond the individual context:
   - Breaks new ground
   - Can be replicated or elaborated

5) The activity or work, both process and product or result, is reviewed and judged to be meritorious and significant by a panel of one's peers.

It will be the responsibility of your academic unit to determine if the activity or work itself falls within the priorities of the department, school/college, discipline, and institution. It will be your responsibility to provide substantiation of the significance and quality of your work.

*Based on* Diamond, R. M. (2002). The mission-driven faculty reward system. In R. M. Diamond (Ed.), *Field guide to academic leadership* (p. 280). San Francisco, CA: Jossey-Bass.

This approach has a number of advantages.

- Individual academic units can be given the responsibility of determining if a specific activity falls within the work of the discipline and the priorities of the institution, school/college, and department.

- The criteria that are used can be relatively clear, easy to understand, and consistent across all disciplines.

- The system is fair and recognizes difference; no one discipline or group of disciplines determines what scholarship should be for another.

- The process is cost-effective. Faculty preparing for review know what is expected of them and the documentation that is required. Faculty serving on review committees can focus on the quality of the product and process and not on whether the activity should be considered scholarly.

- This approach can be incorporated easily into the descriptions of scholarly work developed by Boyer and Rice and the more recent work of Hutchings and Shulman (1999).

In addition, this approach eliminates the need to categorize the activity. While what a faculty member does may represent basic or applied research, be in the context of teaching or service or in the creative arts, the setting is not of prime importance. What is important is that the process that is followed and the resultant outcome represent a level of quality supported by appropriate documentation. While your campus materials and guidelines may not include a definition of scholarship or use this approach, you may have the ability to build on it in your documentation.

It is the role of the academic unit or department to identify those specific areas of work that fall within the priorities of the department, within the context of the discipline, and within the mission and vision of the institution. If you would like to expand the range of activities that are considered as scholarship, start the conversation early with your chair, dean, and committee members. Don't charge ahead only to find out that you have been going down the wrong path.

Some institutions have published statements or guides that help to substantiate activities that are of particular importance in light of institutional missions. For example, the Office of Continuing Education and Public Service at the University of Illinois at Urbana–Champaign has published *A Faculty Guide for Relating Public Service to the Promotion and Tenure Review Process* (1993)[1]. Materials of this type that discuss criteria, documentation, and evaluation in the context of the specific values of the institution can be extremely helpful to both faculty members preparing for review and to the members of the review committee.

## DOCUMENTING TEACHING EFFECTIVENESS

In the evaluation of teaching, four basic questions must be addressed:

- Which characteristics will be evaluated?

- How will data be collected?

- Who will do the evaluation?

- Are you using a portion of your teaching as a scholarly activity?

A number of options exist under each of the first three questions (see Table 2.2). You should also keep in mind, as is true with service, that teaching can indeed be scholarship and that, as Hutchings and Shulman (1999) have so clearly pointed out, there is a distinct difference between the scholarship of teaching and scholarly teaching. Teaching becomes scholarship, they believe, when it is made public, is available for peer review and critique according to accepted standards, and can be reproduced and built on by other scholars.

In particular disciplines, outcomes of instruction may be easier to demonstrate than in others. In general, the dynamic nature of learning makes documentation complicated. Nonetheless, every attempt should be made to focus on ways in which your students' learning can be substantiated and documented. Shifts away from what students say about the teacher and course toward what students are able to demonstrate as a result of their experience in the course are concomitant with shifts in modes of instruction.

Different measures are appropriate for different student/teacher interactions. Keep in mind that reviewing teaching needs to be sensitive to the fact that many of our standard practices for evaluating teaching are based on traditional models of instruction as well as particular assumptions about the role of teacher that contemporary theories call into question. The role of teacher as lecturer and deliverer of knowledge is an anachronism in many institutions or contexts. As the nature of teaching shifts, and as technology becomes more available,

TABLE 2.2

## Documenting Teaching Effectiveness

**Which characteristics will be evaluated?**
- Knowledge and uses of the research on teaching and learning
- Clearly stated learning outcomes with appropriate assessment procedures
- Effective and appropriate use of technology
- Appropriate mix of alternative learning strategies
- Good organization of subject matter and course
- Effective communication
- Knowledge of and enthusiasm for the subject matter and teaching
- Positive attitudes toward students
- Fairness in assessment and grading
- Flexibility in approaches to teaching

**How will data be collected?**
- Self-assessment/report
- Classroom observation
- Structured interview
- Instructional rating survey
- Test or appraisal of student achievement and attitudes
- Content analysis of instructional materials and student manuals
- Review of classroom records
- Alumni survey

**Who will do the evaluating?**
- Self
- Students
- Faculty
- Dean or department chair
- Alumni
- Other appropriate administrators
- Others participating in class-related activities
- Work or internship supervisor

*Modified from* Centra, J., Froh, R. C., Gray, P. J., & Lambert, L. M. (1987). In R. M. Diamond (Ed.), *A guide to teaching for promotion and tenure* (p. 15). Acton, MA: Copley.

the data that you will need to substantiate or document your teaching must shift as well. Your committee should be open to the new roles of faculty members as coaches, facilitators, and co-learners. It will be your responsibility to select the combination of measures that is most appropriate to your own teaching.

## Student Ratings

Although more comprehensive assessment strategies are now emerging, evaluation of teaching has depended heavily in the past on student ratings. Such measures, while useful, provide only one vision of teacher effectiveness. You should keep in mind that student evaluations are usually collected near the end of the term when many of the failing or unhappy students are no longer in attendance or when those who have remained in class are anxious about final grades. Rather than depending solely on student evaluations to demonstrate your effectiveness in the classroom, think about materials you can collect over time that will demonstrate your growth as a teacher and will display the dynamic nature of the learning enterprise. Course syllabi, assignments and other handouts, student papers, tests, exams, and external review of student performance or progress can all be used to demonstrate facets of your teaching.

As you collect information about your teaching, remember that student ratings of your teaching can be used to help improve your effectiveness and show that you have worked to become a better teacher and that you have collected evidence to show improvement. For example, administering a student feedback instrument mid-semester can provide you with useful information that also shows your students that you care about their progress. This practice offers you the opportunity to make immediate changes in your teaching. Using the same instrument at the end of the semester, or at the same time the following year, can provide evidence of improvement.

Most student rating scales are focused on the lecture as an instructional model. If you are teaching a seminar, studio, laboratory, or independent study courses, make sure that inappropriate questions are dropped from student evaluation instruments and replaced with items that address the type of teaching that you do. See Resource 5 in Part II for examples of questions that might be added for different instructional settings.

## Comparative Ratings

If you are going to use student ratings to help show the quality of your teaching, it is very important that you compare your data on an item-by-item basis with the averages for other faculty in your department, school/college, or institution. Since most faculty score "above average" responses, providing these data without comparative information is not particularly meaningful. You should be able to get your department, school/college, and institution means from your chair, dean, or the office that does the processing. A simple graphic, such as the following, can effectively present this information for each of the questions on the instrument.

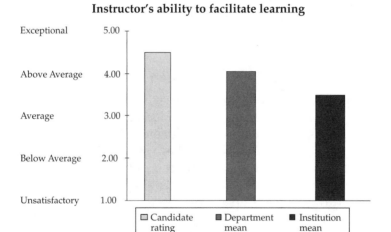

## Teacher-Constructed Materials

If you are experimenting with a new instructional approach or have developed new materials for use in your course, the "mini-quest" can provide you (and later the review committee) with useful information. The mini-quest is given to students immediately after the completion of an intellectual unit (see Resource 3 in Part II). The items can be modified to the specific materials or instructional approaches that you are evaluating. Repeated use of this instrument provides feedback on the quality of the instructional materials and helps document change over time as you revise the approach or materials.

## Documenting Student Learning

It is interesting to note that few faculty include in their documentation evidence of student learning. Such evidence can be some of the most powerful information you can provide. While the dynamic nature of learning makes documentation complicated, you should make every attempt to document the learning that has taken place in your classroom. There are a number of things you can do in this area. If, for example, you have included statements of learning outcomes in your syllabus or course materials, how successful were your students in reaching each of these objectives? What changes have occurred over time? How has student performance improved? The key question to ask yourself is, "If I am successful as a teacher, what impact will it have on my students and what evidence can I present to demonstrate this impact?" See Grunert (1997) if you are preparing an expanded syllabus or resource materials for your course.

## Documenting Other Factors That Can Impact Students

As a faculty member, your teaching can have an impact on students in a variety of areas that can also be documented. For example, has there been an increase in your course enrollment? Has attrition decreased? Have attitudes changed? If you have been involved in a major curriculum revision, has there been an impact on job placement or certification performance or in student placement in graduate schools? If you teach an introductory course, have there been changes in students' success in subsequent courses in your discipline? Has enrollment in these follow-up courses increased? Has the number of majors increased? What do other faculty say? The answers to each of these questions can be included in the data you provide the committee.

## Other Supportive Materials

Quite often candidates leave out key materials that relate directly to the quality of their teaching. These may include a comprehensive student manual (or expanded syllabus) that you have developed for your course(s), case studies, unusual resources, special assignments or activities in the community, and so forth. In those instances you should also include in your portfolio a rationale of why you believe these materials are important. If you can show a direct impact on learning, attitude changes, or course efficiency, their inclusion can be extremely powerful.

## DOCUMENTING TEACHING AS SCHOLARSHIP

As part of your teaching there is a growing probability that you will be involved in some form of innovative activity, ranging from exploring new applications of technology and implementing active, collaborative, or cooperative learning, or a problem-based approach to being responsible for the design, implementation, and evaluation of a revised course. In some instances these activities will meet all of the criteria that describe scholarship as indicated in Table 2.1.

It will be up to you to decide if you wish to select this activity as the focus of your scholarship. If you do take this approach (and this is true of any other nontraditional form of scholarship) you must make sure that:

- The policies of your academic unit permit this.

- You have the support of your chair and dean.

- You document everything: the process, the impact, and how what you are doing builds on research.

- You document each of the problems you are addressing.

When it comes to teaching, remember that there are wide ranges of potential and significant impact areas about which data can be collected. These include:

- Student learning: How has it improved? Where has it improved? How much has it improved? For all or for certain subsets of your population?

- Student attitudes (about the discipline, the topic, etc.): Have they changed? From what to what? If it is a lower-division course, are you having an impact on the number of students who choose your major or select additional courses in your field?

- Attention and retention: As a result of your work, have the figures changed?

- Job placement, enrollment, or increased success in follow-up courses.

- Has there been an impact on the cost of instruction? Increasing the scope of the course without adding time or resources or handling more students for the same cost is significant.

Unless you collect this base information for each of these topics before you begin you will be unable to show change or describe the significance of what you have accomplished.

## DOCUMENTING THE USE AND APPLICATION OF TECHNOLOGY

With each year more applications of technology are finding their way into our teaching, scholarship, and administrative roles. You may be involved in software design, hardware design, or in applying an approach developed in one field to a brand new application in another.

Two chapters in *Field Guide to Academic Leadership* (Diamond, 2002) may be helpful in these areas.

- Chapter 11, "Technology in the Learning Process," provides a review of the basic applications of technology in teaching, a rationale for each application, and links this material to the related research on teaching and learning. There is also a very useful annotated bibliography.

- Chapter 20, "Dealing with Technology: Administrative Issues," addresses the dissemination of technology and its use in administrative applications.

If technology innovation will be a part your portfolio, see Resource 4 in Part II for additional guidelines.

## DOCUMENTING ADVISING EFFECTIVENESS

A growing number of institutions are focusing on advising effectiveness and including the topic in the data that they are collecting from their students.

Most of this information will not be available to you, but you can independently collect some feedback on your advising effectiveness. The following are three basic areas you should address:

- Your availability: How accessible are you? Are you at your office when you say you will be? Do you meet your appointments with your students?

- Your knowledge: How accurate and timely is the information that you provide to your students?

- Your helpfulness: Do your students perceive you as interested and concerned, and is the information that you provide useful in that it meets their particular needs?

Your primary source of information is, of course, your students. However, to these data you should add your own self-evaluation and the perceptions of your peers and chair. Keep in mind that you will be collecting information for two purposes: formative evaluation and summative evaluation. *Formative evaluation* will show improvement and quality. You would include these data in your documentation to show change over time. This is also the information you use to determine if and where improvement is needed. *Summative evaluation* will show how well you are doing. If data are available on other faculty for comparison purposes, all the better.

While the weight given to advising effectiveness may vary considerably from case to case, it is a common category of faculty work. A number of survey instruments have been developed for this purpose and, as with any instrument of this type, it should be used over time so that you can benefit from the information as part of formative evaluation. See Resource 6 in Part II for a segment of a student survey on academic advising.

Check with your student advising office to see if a survey instrument is available on your campus. If you choose to use one available through a professional organization, be sure that it covers the topics of availability, knowledge, and helpfulness and is in line with what your department, school/college, or institution expects of you as an advisor. Your faculty manual will usually include such a statement. For representative survey instruments check with the National Academic Advising Association (NACADA; http://www.nacada.ksu.edu). See Kramer (2003) for more information on evaluating advising and to explore ways to be more effective in this role.

## DOCUMENTING SERVICE

While many faculty activities fall under the category of citizenship, the focus of your documentation must be on the importance of the activities and the quality of the work being performed. The weight given to these activities may vary considerably based on your assignment, the significance of the activity, and the relative weight customarily given to this type of work in promotion and tenure cases on your campus or in your department.

Depending upon disciplinary practice and institutional and unit missions, outreach may be assessed as part of the service or, as in the case of teaching, as the scholarly domain of your work. The scholarly aspects of such work should not be overlooked.

For service to be considered scholarly it must be research based, require a high level of discipline expertise, and move your field ahead. Additionally, the process and its result must have application beyond your own institution and the community. Don't underestimate the criteria of significance. Once again, collecting data about conditions before you implement your new activity or approach is extremely important since it will be the basis for documenting impact. There are many instances where faculty are using their discipline knowledge to serve as consultants and having significant impact on their communities, their states, or the nation.

## DOCUMENTING INTERDISCIPLINARY OR COLLABORATIVE WORK

One of the more complex challenges you will face is documenting both your role and your contributions when you're part of a team composed of other faculty, staff, or, in some instances, individuals from outside of the institution. These projects might be research oriented, might focus on teaching-related initiatives, or be in the context of community or organizational service. Your documentation will be even more complex when this activity is being presented as your scholarly activity.

To collect the necessary information, you must focus on the key questions that will be asked of yourself and other team members. In a number of instances both you and your fellow team members will be answering the same questions. The following is the information you should provide:

- What specific expertise did you bring to the project?

- What was your specific role on the team? Were there certain elements of the project or initiatives where you had a greater role?

- Were certain products developed for which you played a major role? What were they, how was their effect measured, and what were the results?

- What was the significance of the effort? What impact does it or will it have?

- If this initiative is to be used to meet the objective of scholarship, are all the needed characteristics being met?

Your team members should be asked to provide the following information:

- What, from their perspective, was your role on the team?

- Did you bring to the project needed expertise in certain areas? If so, what were they?

- Were you an active and contributing member of the team? Did you work effectively with other team members? Were deadlines met and responsibilities fulfilled?

- What was your major contributions to the effort?

- From their perspective, what was the significance of the effort and its potential impact?

- In the future, would they choose to work with you again on other projects?

This information can be collected by you or by the committee and included in your documentation. Check to see what the committee prefers—it may be a combination of both. If your assignment is inter-disciplinary, make sure that your documentation includes data that represents the view of faculty from each of the disciplines involved.

## POST-TENURE REVIEW

You should not expect the evaluation of your work to end once you obtain tenure. A growing number of campuses have implemented a formal program of post-tenure review. And while the process itself may vary, the rationale behind its reviews and their purpose have much in common.

Licata and Morreale (1997) have made the following observations:

> . . . post-tenure review usually means a systematic, comprehensive process, separate from annual review, aimed specifically at assessing performance and/or nurturing faculty growth and development. This

process is initiated periodically of *all* tenured faculty or
for *certain* tenured faculty as a result of some trigger
event. Or sometimes individual faculty members vol-
unteer for such a review for personal or professional
reasons. (p. 1)

Licata and Morreale also observed that post-tenure review, like
any performance evaluation, has two fundamental purposes: summative—providing accurate information about post performance that is
used to make a personal decision usually in the form of rewind or
remediation—and formative—a review process that focuses on the for-
mulation of a professional development plan emphasizing future
growth. In formative evaluation no final immediate personal action
usually occurs. It is your own institution, based on need, pressures by
external stake holders or internal constituencies, that will determine
the scope and purpose of post-tenure review on your campus. Since
there is such a wide range of procedures in existence, once you have
received tenure, it is important that you determine your institutional
polices and procedures and plan accordingly. If such a post-tenure policy does exist, there are five areas that you should question:

- The stated rationale behind the policy

- If the review process is being applied to everyone or just to
  selected faculty and, if so, how they are selected

- The procedures and timing of the review

- The criteria that will be employed

- Who will be involved

If you participate in such a review, remember that this is a great
way to explore new options and take advantage of new opportunities
to revitalize your academic career. If a post-tenure review is in your
future, prepare for it by collecting key documentation from the start.
You will need base data, and much of this can come from your tenure
review. Don't throw anything out! While it may be difficult at the
beginning to know what you will need, keep collecting data and building a portfolio on your impact and accomplishments. For an excellent
update on post-tenure review at a number of campuses, see Licata and
Morreale (2002).

## THE PROFESSIONAL PORTFOLIO: TYING IT ALL TOGETHER

A professional portfolio brings together all of the work you have done in various areas and presents an overview of your best practices. The professional portfolio is a carefully constructed and organized set of materials that represents the full range of your work. It begins with a reflective essay (described in the following section) and is structured in such a way to assist the committee in understanding your accomplishments and their significance. Documentation of your work in any portfolio should stress two dimensions: the quality of the work and the significance of the work. Faculty often provide promotion and tenure committees with detailed information as to the quality of their effort but neglect to present a case for the value of their work, describing its impact or explaining in what ways and for whom the work has significance. This is extremely important because there is a growing inclination on the part of committees to focus on why the activity was undertaken in the first place and why it is important.

Your documents can be collected from a number of sources. What is important is that the material be focused and manageable. A "selected" professional portfolio, as the name implies, provides a selection of materials that can be reviewed in depth. However, before you take this approach make sure that it will meet the expectations of your committee. Some committees will, following their institution's guidelines, be required to ask for far more than they really need.

Table 2.3 provides a list of potential sources of documentation. Notice that while the committee may request additional information in certain categories, you can provide basic documentation in every one.

A growing number of institutions provide their faculty with specific guidelines to use as they develop their teaching or professional portfolio and with professional support through a faculty or institutional development office. The Center for Teaching Excellence at Texas A&M University (http://www.tamu.edu/cte/sermain.htm), the Center for Teaching Excellence at The Ohio State University (http://www.acs.ohio-state.edu/education/ftad/portfolio/), and the Center for Effective Teaching and Learning at the University of Texas–El Paso (http://www.utep.edu/cetal/portfoli/) all have produced guidelines on developing the teaching section of your portfolio. Many institutional resource libraries have a wealth of information on this subject and have staff that will assist faculty with data collection and portfolio development.

TABLE 2.3

**Potential Sources of Documentation**

---

**Establishing quality**

- Expert testimony (formal reviews, juries, and solicited testimony)
- Faculty essay (describing the process that was followed, the rationale behind the decisions that were made, and the quality of the products)
- Formal reports and studies
- Publications, displays, or presentations (videotaped)

**Establishing significance**

- Faculty essay (explaining why the work is important, to whom, and for what purposes)
- External reviews focusing on the significance and usefulness of the activity or product
- Impact on the intended audience
  - ~ Size and scope
  - ~ Documentation (changes in learning, attitudes, performance)
- Relation to the mission statement of the institution/department
- Documentation of individual assignment (what does your department require)

---

One of the most widely used references on teaching portfolios is Peter Seldin's *The Teaching Portfolio* (2004). See Resource 8 in Part II for guidelines to assist you with the narrative portions of your portfolio.

## THE FACULTY ESSAY

The reflective statement is the initial document in your materials and an excellent source of information for the review committee. This descriptive essay may have a number of functions, but its primary purpose is to provide a frame of reference or context for the items submitted to the committee. It describes what you see as your priorities and strengths, it states your case, and it provides important information to the committee that would not otherwise be available, such as:

- A description of issues from your perspective
- A rationale for choices that you made
- The extent to which your expectations were met
- Circumstances that promoted or inhibited success
- The significance of this work as an intellectual contribution, from your perspective
- An organizational framework for the materials you are submitting—the rationale behind the organization of your materials

For example, if you have written a textbook, how is it different from other textbooks on the market and why is this an important distinction? If you have directed a play, what specific issues were you addressing, and how is your solution different or unique; why is this important? If you were trying something new, why was this effort important, and if it was not completely successful, what did you learn and how would you modify what you did? Keep in mind that you are the *only* source for this information.

The faculty essay can—and this is a most important benefit—also serve as the basis for the specific questions that the committee will ask of external reviewers, thus focusing their attention on the issues you and the committee feel are most important. The essay can be used as a descriptive document that provides a rationale for the materials that you have forwarded to the committee and is one way for you to demonstrate a capacity to be reflective and self-critical, hence, capable of continued growth and change.

The faculty essay also provides a vehicle for discussion of special circumstances that have affected your work to date or its review. If, for example, you have been caught in a political struggle within your department and you believe this dispute led to mixed reviews of your work by your colleagues, you may want to address this situation in your essay. Since such disclosures have associated risks, think your decision through carefully. In certain situations, such discussions can advance your case by providing insight your reviewers would not otherwise glean.

It is important, however, to remember the distinction between the descriptive essay and the work itself. You will be judged on the quality of your work. The descriptive essay enhances reviewers' understanding of your work and provides them with a structure to follow, but it does not replace the documentation. It may also prove helpful to ask a colleague to review and edit your essay as well as any other documents you have written. Often a fresh pair of eyes can pick up obvious, but overlooked, errors.

## EXAMPLES OF DOCUMENTATION

The National Project on Institutional Priorities and Faculty Rewards, coordinated at Syracuse University, used faculty teams from several campuses and a range of disciplines to consider a number of cases and suggest ways in which specific activities might be documented for promotion and tenure review. Several such examples are found in Resource 7 in Part II. As you review these examples, please keep in mind that they are illustrative and not intended to be prescriptive in their detail. You may want to ask your department head or chair of your committee if any examples of successful documentation or strategies are available for you to consult. Some departments collect review materials to share with faculty as part of a formal mentoring plan.

## IN SUMMARY

Preparing for promotion and tenure review is not an easy task. It takes time, planning, and a great deal of hard work. You can be sure that your colleagues on the committee will try to be as fair and supportive as possible. As the candidate, you have the opportunity to help them in their role by providing them with a carefully constructed collection of materials on which to base their decision.

If your campus has a three-year review, use it as a base for the full review that will take place several years later. Use the materials included in your annual review to show improvements over time. The comments and advice you receive from your chair and other faculty can prove to be extremely helpful as you move ahead. As hard as some comments may be to take, remember that the purpose of the advice is to guide you. Failures, if used as learning experiences, can be viewed in a positive way. For example, a teaching practice that did not work at first can be a powerful asset if you show that you identified a problem or issue, dealt with it, and succeeded in learning from it. If you are fortunate enough to have a senior faculty member serving as your mentor, ask questions, get reactions, and make maximum use of this most valuable resource.

Don't lose sight of the fact that the success of your review is, for the most part, in your hands. Be proactive—start collecting your data early, identify the questions you might be asked, and begin to build your case. Preparing for review is an ongoing process. Remember your audience. Prepare your materials so that they can be understood and appreciated by anyone who is asked to review them. You can make the process of personnel reviews less stressful and more productive by being prepared. Your future in higher education is in your hands. I wish you well.

## Endnote

[1]Single copies are available at no charge by writing to the Office of Continuing Education and Public Service, University of Illinois, 302 E. John Street, Suite 202, Champaign, IL 61820.

### REFERENCES

American Historical Association Ad Hoc Committee on Redefining Scholarly Work. (1993). *Redefining historical scholarship.* Washington, DC: American Historical Association. Retrieved November 17, 2003, from http://www.theaha.org/pubs/redef.htm

Association of American Medical Colleges. (2000). *Redefining scholarship in contemporary academic medicine: Essays on scholarship sponsored by the AAMC Council of Academic Societies.* Washington, DC: Author.

Boyer, E. L. (1990). *Scholarship reconsidered: Priorities of the professoriate.* Princeton, NJ: The Carnegie Foundation for the Advancement of Teaching.

Centra, J., Froh, R. C., Gray, P. J., & Lambert, L. M. (1987). In R. M. Diamond (Ed.), *A guide to evaluating teaching for promotion and tenure.* Acton, MA: Copley.

Diamond, R. M. (1999). *Aligning faculty rewards with institutional mission: Statements, policies, and guidelines.* Bolton, MA: Anker.

Diamond, R. M. (Ed.). (2002). *Field guide to academic leadership.* San Francisco, CA: Jossey-Bass.

Diamond, R. M., & Adam, B. E. (Eds.). (1993). *New directions in higher education: No. 81. Recognizing faculty work: Reward systems for the year 2000.* San Francisco, CA: Jossey-Bass.

Diamond, R. M., & Adam, B. E. (Eds.). (1995). *The disciplines speak: Rewarding the scholarly, professional, and creative work of faculty.* Washington, DC: American Association for Higher Education.

Diamond, R. M., & Adam, B. E. (Eds.). (2000). *The disciplines speak II: More statements on rewarding the scholarly, professional, and creative work of faculty.* Washington, DC: American Association for Higher Education.

Gardiner, L. F. (1994). *Redesigning higher education: Producing dramatic gains in student learning* (ASHE-ERIC Higher Education Report No. 7). Washington, DC: George Washington University, Graduate School of Education and Human Development.

Glassick, C. E., Huber, M. T., & Maeroff, G. I. (1997). *Scholarship assessed: Evaluation of the professoriate*. San Francisco, CA: Jossey-Bass.

Gray, P., Adam, B., Diamond, R., Froh, R., & Yonai, B. (1994). Defining, assigning, and assessing faculty work. In M. Kinnick (Ed.), *New directions for institutional research: No. 84. Providing useful information for deans and department chairs*. San Francisco, CA: Jossey-Bass.

Grunert, J. (1997). *The course syllabus: A learning-centered approach*. Bolton, MA: Anker.

Hutchings, P., & Shulman, L. S. (1999, September/October). The scholarship of teaching: New elaborations, new developments. *Change, 31*(5), 11–15.

Kramer, G. L. (Ed.). (2003). *Faculty advising examined: Enhancing the potential of college faculty as advisors*. Bolton, MA: Anker.

Licata, C. M., & Morreale, J. C. (1997). *Post-tenure review: Policies, practices, precautions*. Washington, DC: American Association for Higher Education.

Licata, C. M., & Morreale, J. C. (Eds.). (2002). *Post-tenure faculty review and renewal: Experienced voices*. Washington, DC: American Association for Higher Education.

National Education Association. (1994). *Entering the profession: Advice for the untenured*. Washington, DC: Author.

Office of Continuing Education and Public Service. (1993). *A faculty guide for relating public service to the promotion and tenure review process*. Urbana, IL: University of Illinois at Urbana–Champaign.

Seldin, P. (2004). *The teaching portfolio: A practical guide to improved performance and promotion/tenure decisions* (3rd ed.). Bolton, MA: Anker.

Whicker, M. L., Kronenfeld, J. J., & Strickland, R. A. (1993). *Getting tenure*. Thousand Oaks, CA: Sage.

## RECOMMENDED READING

Fink, L. D. (2003). *Creating significant learning experiences: An integrated approach to designing college courses.* San Francisco, CA: Jossey-Bass.

Gelmon, S., & Agre-Kippenhan, S. (2002, January). Promotion, tenure, and the engaged scholar: Keeping the scholarship of engagement in the review process. *AAHE Bulletin, 54*(5), 7–11.

Gordon, V. N., Habley, W. R., & Associates. (2000). *Academic advising: A comprehensive handbook.* San Francisco, CA: Jossey-Bass.

Rice, R. E. (1991). The new American scholar: Scholarship and the purpose of the university. *Metropolitan University Journal, 1*(4), 7–18

# PART II
# RESOURCES

# 1

# ASSESSING COLLEGIALITY: A FACULTY SURVEY

| | Always | Usually | Some-times | Occasion-ally | Never |
|---|---|---|---|---|---|
| **1) Relationship with others** | | | | | |
| a) Interacts with colleagues | 5 | 4 | 3 | 2 | 1 |
| b) Interacts in a positive manner | 5 | 4 | 3 | 2 | 1 |
| c) Engages in give and take of ideas and perspectives | 5 | 4 | 3 | 2 | 1 |
| d) Treats others as professional equals by respecting their ideas, perspectives, and experiences | 5 | 4 | 3 | 2 | 1 |
| **2) Institutional citizen** | | | | | |
| a) Takes his or her turn in doing some of the needed institutional/citizenship responsibilities | 5 | 4 | 3 | 2 | 1 |
| b) Helps others understand the issues and possible solutions to improve the institution | 5 | 4 | 3 | 2 | 1 |

| | | | | | |
|---|---|---|---|---|---|
| c) Uses his or her expertise to respond to institutional needs or problems | 5 | 4 | 3 | 2 | 1 |
| d) Helps develop an environment of open exchange and willingness to help resolve institutional problems/issues | 5 | 4 | 3 | 2 | 1 |
| e) Represents the institution in a professional manner— honest, factual, advocates for its functions, and projects a positive image | 5 | 4 | 3 | 2 | 1 |

| | Very High | High | Aver-age | Fair | Poor |
|---|---|---|---|---|---|
| **3) Overall rating as a colleague** | 5 | 4 | 3 | 2 | 1 |

Developed by Daniel Wheeler, University of Nebraska

# 2

# Documenting Effectiveness and Impact as a Member of a Team

If you have been involved in a team project that you believe is an important element in your review, you should include the following information:

- Title of the project

- Was the project funded externally or by your institution? If externally, who was the sponsor?

- If the project was undertaken with a specific charge to your team, what was the charge?

- Who were the other members of your team (provide address, phone and fax numbers, and email)?

- What were the specific problem(s) you were addressing as a team?

- What was your role on the team?

- What specific disciplinary expertise or other strengths did you bring to the project?

- Were there specific elements of the project in which you played a major role? What were they?

- Were you the (or a) primary author of specific materials? If so, what were they? Are they available for committee review?

- What was the impact of the project and how has it been determined?

**Important:** If this project is being presented as a major scholarly, professional, or creative activity, describe the process that was followed and the results of the initiative. Impact and significance should be documented following the guidelines in Chapter 2.

# 3

# MINI-QUEST: QUESTIONNAIRE FOR EVALUATING AN INSTRUCTIONAL UNIT

Student Evaluation of an Instructional Unit

Date _____ Material Title _____

Course Title _____Instructor _____

Please circle the most appropriate alternative.

1) INTEREST
   This unit was:
   (1) very uninteresting
   (2) uninteresting
   (3) interesting
   (4) very interesting

2) PACE
   This unit was:
   (1) much too fast
   (2) a little too fast
   (3) just right
   (4) a little too slow
   (5) much too slow

3) LEARNING
   I learned:
   (1) nothing
   (2) very little
   (3) a fair amount
   (4) a great deal

4) CLARITY
   The unit was:
   (1) very unclear
   (2) unclear
   (3) clear
   (4) very clear

5) IMPORTANCE
   What I learned was:
   (1) very unimportant
   (2) unimportant
   (3) important
   (4) very important

6) GENERAL
   Generally, these materials were:
   (1) poor
   (2) fair
   (3) good
   (4) excellent

7)   Please indicate any questions raised by the unit.


8)   Please write at least one specific comment here about the unit. (Use the back if necessary.)

Thank you!


Revised from Diamond, R. M. (1989). *Designing and improving courses and curricula in higher education.* San Francisco, CA. Jossey-Bass.

# 4

# Documenting an Instructional Innovation or Use of Technology: Guidelines for Faculty

1) What was the specific problem you were addressing (unmet instructional goals, high drop-out or failure rate, reduced enrollment, attitudinal problems, poor attendance, poor participation in class, etc.)? Please document if data is available.

2) What specific innovations did you employ? What instructional materials or software did you use? What did you do differently?

3) Did you have any financial or professional support? (If so, what kind and from what source?) If you worked with other faculty, what was your specific role?

4) Why did you do what you did? (Did you base your approach on reports, articles, research, etc.? If so what were they?)

5) What happened?
   - Were your goals reached? What supportive data do you have?
   - What did you learn? What worked, what didn't, and why?
   - Did you have any unintended outcomes? (Did it take more or less of your time or your students' time than you expected? Were there any financial, space, or equipment surprises, etc.?)

6) Will you continue to use this approach?
   - If so, will you do anything differently?
   - If not, why not?

7) Will you be reporting what you did to others in your field? If so, how?

# 5

# STUDENT RATINGS OF FACULTY: SPECIAL INSTRUCTIONAL SETTINGS (SELECTED EXAMPLES)

## Laboratory

- To what extent did the assignments relate to course outcomes and goals?
- Were the laboratory activities coordinated with other work in the course?
- Was the instructor prepared for laboratory sessions and pre-activity discussions?
- Were you provided with adequate instructions for proceeding with your laboratory exercises?
- Did you have enough time in the laboratory to complete your exercises?

## Studio

- Were you exposed to a variety of techniques and procedures?
- Did the instructor take time to work with you individually?
- Were the instructor's examples/demonstrations clear and concise?
- Did you have enough time to develop the skills you needed to succeed?
- Were the instructor's critiques of your work useful? Did you learn from them?

- Was the instructor sensitive to your problems?
- Did your instructor help you think about different ways to approach projects?

## Team Teaching

- Did one instructor dominate the course?
- Were the faculty involved in teaching the course compatible with each other?
- Did the involvement of more than one faculty member provide you with insights that a single faculty member could not?
- Was the instruction in the course coordinated?

## Internship/Clinical

- Were you exposed to a variety of problems?
- Was the experience realistic?
- Were your questions thoroughly answered?
- Were problems clearly stated?
- Was evaluation consistent?
- Were appropriate and inappropriate clinical procedures/ approaches clearly identified and discussed?
- Was your faculty member available when needed

These examples are based, in part, on items included in the Instructor and Course Evaluation System developed at the University of Illinois at Urbana–Champaign. See http://www.oir.uiuc.edu/dme/Ices/index.htm for more information.

# EVALUATING AN ADVISOR: SELECTED ITEMS FROM THE ACT SURVEY OF ACADEMIC ADVISING

| | DOES NOT APPLY | STRONGLY AGREE | AGREE | NEUTRAL | DISAGREE | STRONGLY DISAGREE |
|---|---|---|---|---|---|---|
| 19. Allows sufficient time to discuss issues or problems. | 0 | 0 | 0 | 0 | 0 | 0 |
| 20. Is willing to discuss personal problems. | 0 | 0 | 0 | 0 | 0 | 0 |
| 21. Anticipates my needs. | 0 | 0 | 0 | 0 | 0 | 0 |
| 22. Helps me select courses that match my interests and abilities. | 0 | 0 | 0 | 0 | 0 | 0 |
| 23. Helps me to examine my needs, interests, and values. | 0 | 0 | 0 | 0 | 0 | 0 |
| 24. Is familiar with my academic background. | 0 | 0 | 0 | 0 | 0 | 0 |
| 25. Encourages me to talk about myself and my college experiences. | 0 | 0 | 0 | 0 | 0 | 0 |
| 26. Encourages my interest in an academic discipline. | 0 | 0 | 0 | 0 | 0 | 0 |
| 27. Encourages my involvement in extracurricular activities. | 0 | 0 | 0 | 0 | 0 | 0 |
| 28. Helps me explore careers in my field of interest. | 0 | 0 | 0 | 0 | 0 | 0 |
| 29. Is knowledgeable about courses outside my major area of study. | 0 | 0 | 0 | 0 | 0 | 0 |
| 30. Seems to enjoy advising. | 0 | 0 | 0 | 0 | 0 | 0 |
| 31. Is approachable and easy to talk to. | 0 | 0 | 0 | 0 | 0 | 0 |
| 32. Shows concern for my personal growth and development. | 0 | 0 | 0 | 0 | 0 | 0 |
| 33. Keeps personal information confidential. | 0 | 0 | 0 | 0 | 0 | 0 |
| 34. Is flexible in helping me plan my academic program. | 0 | 0 | 0 | 0 | 0 | 0 |
| 35. Has a sense of humor. | 0 | 0 | 0 | 0 | 0 | 0 |
| 36. Is a helpful, effective advisor whom I would recommend to other students. | 0 | 0 | 0 | 0 | 0 | 0 |

For information on the use of this instrument contact:
ACT
500 ACT Drive
P.O. Box 168, Iowa City, IA 52243-0168
(319) 337-1000

# 7

# Documenting and Assessing the Work of Faculty: Selected Examples

## Example 1

### Authoring a Textbook as a Fundamental Introduction to the Discipline

*Rationale*

- Demonstrates a high level of understanding of the field, ability to integrate knowledge, and ability to represent knowledge to others (and thus a teaching skill)

- May represent knowledge that is put together in creative or novel ways leading to new insights

- Integrates teaching and scholarly aspects of faculty role

- Has the potential to lead to future scholarship

- Makes teaching public—cosmopolitan—beyond the bounds of campus

- Helps other faculty think of different ways of organizing and presenting information

- May improve student learning and attitudes toward the discipline

## Suggested Guidelines for Documentation

*Evidence*

- Descriptive essay: should include a statement of existing need, a discussion of how the text represents a new approach or paradigm, and the developmental process that was followed

- Product itself

- Reviews from publisher (during selection process)

- Published reviews

- Student assessments

- Sales (overall and by institution and type)

- Citations (where appropriate)

- Data on student learning and attitudes toward the discipline

- Enrollment in follow-up courses and programs

*Criteria*

- Marketability fills an important or unique niche; levels of adoption

- Quality, accuracy, clarity of content (peers)

- Presentation, style, learning impact (students)

- Impact on how the subject is taught

- Degree of innovation (structure, content, and/or presentation)

- Epistemological impact; how knowledge is structured

- Student learning and attitudes toward the discipline are improved

- Demonstrates scholarly process

## Example 2

## Developing a New School Curriculum

*Rationale*

- Demonstrates the ability to communicate important concepts to a diverse population
- Can increase general student interest in the field
- Can prepare students for further study in the discipline
- Can represent a major new approach to education in the discipline
- Can improve student knowledge
- Can improve student's interest in the subject

## Suggested Guidelines for Documentation

*Evidence*

- Descriptive essay: includes a statement of need, goals of the project, the design process that was followed, and the rationale for the approach being used
- Reviews by experts in the field (college and secondary) and by teachers who are using the materials produced
- The materials
- Data on changes in student learning and attitudes
- Data on the feasibility of continued and expanded use (cost, etc.)
- Data on student learning and attitudes
- Enrollment and attrition data

*Criteria*

- Represents a major innovation
- Quality and accuracy of content
- Meets specific needs of student population being served
- Has application beyond test site (adoption by other schools)

- Validated by an independent review process
- Met other needs that were identified (updating of context, correcting deficiencies, high failure rate, lack of interest in discipline, etc.)
- Demonstrates scholarly process

## Example 3

### Directing a Play (Student Production)

*Rationale*

- Interpretation of the work involves research, creativity, and scholarship

- Requires disciplinary expertise and a historical frame of reference

- Requires the ability to make maximum use of existing resources (human and material)

- Provides theory/practice application for students in the cast and those serving in other production-related roles (teaching function)

### Suggested Guidelines for Documentation

*Evidence*

- Descriptive essay: includes a statement of artistic, intellectual, and production goals; a description of the intellectual and/or production processes; and a rationale for the basic decisions that were made

- Videotape of final production for external peer review

- Critical reviews

- Students' evaluation and critique based on preestablished goals for learning (participants and audience)

- Increased student knowledge about the field, the author, and the social context in which he or she worked

- Instructional format based on research in teaching and learning

*Criteria*

- Shows evidence of a high level of disciplinary expertise

- Makes maximum use of existing resources

- Production is innovative, breaks new ground
- Demonstrates student learning (both participants and audience)
- Can be replicated
- Demonstrates scholarly process

## Example 4

### Designing a New Course

*Rationale*

- Requires a high level of disciplinary expertise

- Can have major impact on student motivation, learning, retention, and attitudes toward the field of study. Can also increase interest of high quality students to major in field

- By improving learning, meets the stated goals of department, school/college, and institution

- Can help prepare students for other courses in the field and for successful careers

## Suggested Guidelines for Documentation

*Evidence*

- Descriptive essay: includes a statement of need and a rationale for the design, the process that was followed, and the rationale behind the decisions that were made (use of the research on teaching and learning)

- Syllabi or student manuals

- Newly created course materials

- Revised structure, change in role of faculty or students, appropriate applications of technology

- Video of class presentation (use of innovative teaching strategies)

- Student ratings

- Student performance data (tests and test results); focus on specific population, if appropriate

- Comments regarding student preparation from faculty teaching high-level courses in the discipline

- Reviews of course and materials by experts in the field (faculty and/or professionals)

- Results of field tests and revisions based on these data
- Comparative data on retention, class attendance, student attitudes, number of students selecting further study in the field
- Improved use of faculty and student time

*Criteria*

- Shows high level of disciplinary expertise
- Represents an innovation or new approach in design, delivery, or content that can be replicated
- Learning outcomes are clearly stated and match the course objectives
- Assessment measures stated outcomes
- Meets the needs of the student population being served and the stated instructional goals
- Is approved by the department and curriculum committee
- Improvements in retention
- Enrollment increases
- Demonstrates scholarly process

## Example 5

## Serving on a Community Task Force
## Appointed by City Mayor

*Rationale*

- Requires a high level of disciplinary expertise

- Can have major impact on reducing conflict within the community

- Fits within the institutional mission statement regarding community service

- Can be used as a case study for classroom use or further research

- Can change attitudes of community leaders and the general public

- Can improve the quality of life in the community

## Suggested Guidelines for Documentation

*Evidence*

- Reflective essay: describes the problems being faced, the role of the faculty member, what the faculty member learned or discovered, and describes the process that was followed and the options that were selected

- Describes barriers that were encountered and how they were overcome

- Description of specific actions the faculty member took as part of the task force and the reasons for those choices

- Transcripts or minutes of task force meetings

- Letters of commendation by the task force chair or members focusing on the specific role played and his or her impact

- Written testimony from community groups who benefited from the work of the task force

- Course materials developed from this case

- Student interaction with faculty member's work or responses to case
- Institutional or unit goal statement articulating community service mission
- Committee interviews with key actors, mayor, community leaders, and so forth
- Results of task force work as evidence of impact on community (i.e., specific initiatives planned and accomplished)
- Publication and dissemination of reports

## Criteria

- Demonstrates a high level of professional expertise
- Demonstrates knowledge of recent research in conflict resolution
- Demonstrates strong performance as a task force member
- Demonstrates innovative solutions to common societal problems
- Demonstrates sensitivity to various constituencies
- Interest in results and outcomes from other communities
- Publication of accounts of activity in news and other media
- Publication of accounts in disciplinary journals
- Changes in laws and policies
- Implementation of recommendations
- Demonstrates scholarly process

## Example 6

## Assisting a Regional Museum in Producing an Exhibit on Indians of the American Southwest (Historian)

*Rationale*

- Requires a high level of disciplinary expertise
- Involves both original research and a new conceptualization of the history and culture of the region
- Requires expertise in pedagogical theory and methodology
- Fits within the institutional mission of community service
- Fits within the institutional mission to support cultural diversity

### Suggested Guidelines for Documentation

*Evidence*

- Descriptive essay: describes the problems being faced, the goals of the exhibit, its contributions to both research and teaching, and a the design process that was followed
- Exhibit script and related publications
- Statement of educational goals and report on visitor evaluation
- Peer reviews of the exhibit
- Data on learning improvements and attitude changes
- Data from others who were involved in the project

*Criteria*

- Shows a high level of disciplinary expertise
- Is innovative in conceptualization and presentation
- Is instructionally effective
- Approach can be applied by others

- Demonstrates ability to work effectively as a team member
- Demonstrates ability to be sensitive to the educational level of the intended audience
- Demonstrates scholarly process

## Example 7

## Developing a Software System to Model
## Storm Water Runoff in an Urban Environment

*Rationale*

- Addresses a major environmental problem

- Demonstrates a high level of disciplinary expertise

- Demonstrates a high level of competence in computer programming

- Demonstrates a high level of competence in environmental modeling

- Improving the design process can reduce costs, improve decision-making, improve safety, reduce flood damage

## Suggested Guidelines for Documentation

*Evidence*

- Software package, including manual that details assumptions, limitations, etc.

- Descriptive essay: should describe the problems being faced (i.e., statement of need), design rationale, benefits of the system, and what makes it an innovative approach

- Published reports and statements for users

- Data on applications (number of users and range of applications)

- Research data on impact (cost reductions in design, savings from reduced damage, etc.)

*Criteria*

- Marketability meets a defined need

- Quality of the system (external reviews)

- Adaptations and use of the system (national and international use)
- Impact of use (reduced costs, reduction in damage, etc.)
- Degree of innovation
- Demonstrates scholarly process

# 8

# THE TEACHING PORTFOLIO: NARRATIVE GUIDELINES FOR FACULTY

Your answers to the questions below will help form the basis of the narrative portions of your portfolio that deal with teaching. After you have gathered the relevant raw materials (see Table 2.2), use these questions as a guide. Describe your accomplishments and include details and examples where appropriate. Remember to be both selective and structured.

1) What are your teaching responsibilities? (Include your courses as well as any other teaching you do.)

2) How would you describe your teaching style and methods? Why do you teach as you do? Give examples and reasons.

3) What would you say your teaching strengths are? What are you most successful at and why? Examples?

4) How do you use course assignments, group work, email, or other tools to foster student learning? What is your emphasis in using these tools (e.g., integrating subject matter with students' experiences, motivating students to engage with the subject matter, giving students hands-on active learning experiences)?

5) What have you done to become a more effective teacher?

   • List teaching workshops attended (topic, presenter, date, brief statement of impact on your teaching).

   • Informal classroom research you have conducted to evaluate and improve your teaching (e.g., one-minute papers, feedback cards, mid-semester evaluation, student journals, student evaluation teams). Be specific and include a statement of how the feedback affected your teaching.

- Your presentations, seminars, and publications on teaching in your discipline (list these as you do on your CV, annotating or providing details as necessary).

6) How do you stay current in the pedagogy of your discipline? How do you translate what you learn into your teaching?

7) What do others (colleagues, administrators, students, alumni, employers of graduates of your courses, etc.) say about your teaching?

Adapted from Seldin, P. (2004). *The teaching portfolio: A practical guide to improved performance and promotion/tenure decisions* (3rd ed.). Bolton, MA: Anker.

*9*

# EVALUATING TEACHING:
# SELECTED ADDITIONAL REFERENCES

Anderson, E. (Ed.). (1993). *Campus use of the teaching portfolio: Twenty-five profiles.* Washington, DC: American Association for Higher Education.

Arreola, R. A. (2000). *Developing a comprehensive faculty evaluation system: A handbook for college faculty and administrators on designing and operating a comprehensive faculty evaluation system* (2nd ed.). Bolton, MA: Anker.

Brookhart, S. M. (2000). *The art and science of classroom assessment: The missing part of pedagogy.* San Francisco, CA: Jossey-Bass.

Braskamp, L. A., & Ory, J. C. (1994). *Assessing faculty work: Enhancing individual and institutional performance.* San Francisco, CA: Jossey-Bass.

Chism, N. V. N. (1999). *Peer review of teaching: A sourcebook.* Bolton, MA: Anker.

Davis, B. G. (1993). *Tools for teaching.* San Francisco, CA: Jossey-Bass.

Edgerton, R., Hutchings, P., & Quinlan, K. (1991). *The teaching portfolio: Capturing the scholarship in teaching.* Washington, DC: American Association for Higher Education.

Elman, S. E., & Smock, S. M. (1985). *Professional service and faculty rewards: Toward an integrated structure.* Washington, DC: National Association of State Universities and Land-Grant Colleges.

Gardiner, L. F., Anderson, C., & Cambridge, B. L. (1997). *Learning through assessment: A resource guide for higher education.* Washington, DC: American Association for Higher Education.

McKeachie, W. J., & Associates (2002). *Teaching tips: Strategies, research, and theory for college and university teachers* (11th ed.). Lexington, MA: D. C. Heath.

Office of Continuing Education and Public Service. (1993). *A faculty guide for relating public service to the promotion and tenure review process.* Urbana, IL: University of Illinois at Urbana–Champaign.

Palomba C. A., & Banta T. W. (1999). *Assessment essentials: Planning, implementing, and improving assessment in higher education.* San Francisco, CA: Jossey-Bass.

Rice, R. E. (1991). The new American scholar: Scholarship and the purposes of the university. *Metropolitan Universities Journal, 1*(4), 7–18.

Ryan, K. E. (2000). New directions for teaching and learning: No. 83. *Evaluating teaching in higher education: A vision for the future.* San Francisco, CA: Jossey-Bass.

Seagren, A. T., Creswell, J. W., & Wheeler, D. W. (2000). *The department chair: New roles, responsibilities, and challenges.* San Francisco, CA: Jossey-Bass.

Seldin, P. (2004). *The teaching portfolio: A practical guide to improved performance and promotion/tenure decisions* (3rd ed.). Bolton, MA: Anker.

Seldin, P., & Associates. (1999). *Changing practices in evaluating teaching: A practical guide to improved faculty performance and promotion/tenure decisions.* Bolton, MA: Anker.

Shulman, L. S. (1989, June). Toward a pedagogy of substance. *AAHE Bulletin, 41*(10), 8–13.

# 10

## PREPARING FOR PROMOTION, TENURE, AND ANNUAL REVIEW: A FACULTY CHECKLIST

### Basic Requirements

Have you included all the items required by your department and school/college guidelines?

Are your materials in logical and appropriate order? Does the sequence make sense?

### Cover Letter or Faculty Essay

Does your cover letter or faculty essay provide guidelines that will help the committee review your materials? Have you discussed:

- The significance of your work from your perspective?

- The challenges you faced and what you accomplished?

- The decisions you made and why you made them?

- The circumstances that promoted or inhibited success?

- The rationale for the materials you have included in your documentation?

- The relationship of your work to the priorities of your department, school/college, institution, and discipline?

## Teaching

In documenting the quality of your teaching have you:

- Presented evidence of quality planning and course design (course organization)?

- Presented evidence of student learning?

- Presented evidence of improvements from semester to semester and from year to year?

- Included student ratings showing comparison with other faculty?

- Included student ratings showing evidence of improvement (where appropriate)?

- Showed evidence of effective, appropriate instructional techniques (use of the research on teaching and learning)?

- Showed evidence of positive impact on retention?

- Included exemplary instructional materials that you have developed?

## Scholarly/Professional/Creative Work

- If you have conducted research and/or published, have you documented the quality and the significance of this work?

- Have you documented the process you followed?

- Have you included statements from qualified external reviewers?

- If appropriate, have you included videos of performance or related activities or included other appropriate visual materials?

- Have you documented how much your activity meets the criteria for scholarly work in your discipline?

- If you have developed innovative instructional materials or written a textbook, have you included external reviews or student performance data that address both the significance and the quality of your work? Have you described how these materials are different from what already exists?

## Advising

- Have you documented the quality of your advising?

## Community Service

- Have you documented service, outreach, or citizenship (department, school/college, institution, community)?

## General

- Have you eliminated all redundant material?
- Have you related what you have done to published research and referenced this material?
- Have you prepared your material in a way that will communicate effectively with colleagues from other disciplines?
- Have you included a table of contents to assist the committee in locating specific items?
- Have you had someone else review your materials?
- Have you collected and used material from your annual review to show growth and improvement over time?

# INDEX